# Recorder *from the* Beginning

## Book 2

### John Pitts

Published by
**EJA Publications**

Exclusive Distributors:

**Hal Leonard**
7777 West Bluemound Road
Milwaukee, WI 53213
Email: info@halleonard.com

**Hal Leonard Europe Limited**
42 Wigmore Street
Marylebone, London, W1U 2RN
Email: info@halleonardeurope.com

**Hal Leonard Australia Pty. Ltd.**
4 Lentara Court
Cheltenham, Victoria, 3192 Australia
Email: info@halleonard.com.au

## Acknowledgements

The publishers would like to thank the following for permission to include copyright material:

'Down In Bethlehem' (Holdstock) reproduced by kind permission of Jan Holdstock. All Rights Reserved.

'The Fireman's Not For Me' (MacColl) ©Stormking Music Inc. Administered in the UK & Eire by
Harmony Music Ltd, Onward House, 11 Uxbridge Street, London W8 7TQ.

Illustrations by Tom Wanless.

Design by Butterworth Design.

Music processing and layout by Camden Music.

This recorder course in three stages has been designed for children aged 7 upwards. Since publication it has become one of the most popular schemes used in many parts of the world.

*Recorder from the Beginning* assumes no previous knowledge of either music or the recorder, and full explanations are provided at every stage so that specialist teaching is not essential. Teacher's Books are available for each stage, and these contain simple piano accompaniments, guitar chord symbols and suggestions for each tune, often using pitched/ unpitched percussion.

All three Pupil's Books are also available in Book & CD editions (CDs not available separately) and the recorded accompaniments will enhance any level of practice or performance, whether by beginners or advanced players. They include a model version of each tune (except in Book 3), followed by exciting, stylish accompaniments for recorders to play along with, both in school and at home.

Revision of the original books for the new full-colour edition has allowed me to make various changes to improve the scheme. The eight extra pages in Book 1 have allowed for some new tunes and rounds, whilst retaining the well-known favourites that have helped to make the scheme such an enduring success. Book 2 has 13 new items as well as new optional duets. Book 3 has the most changes of all, to allow for the introduction of 27 new pieces. I have also made a small change to the order of introducing new notes.

For all these changes in the different books we have recorded exciting new accompaniment tracks for the CDs, plus improved tracks for some of the previous pieces. I have also strengthened and increased the optional opportunities for recorder players to contribute to music units in the National Curriculum, by combining their recorder playing with class music activities such as singing and the use of pitched and unpitched percussion.

I know you will enjoy the lovely pictures created by Tom Wanless, and I wish to thank Tom for his stunning contribution. I also wish to thank my wife Maureen for her never-ending support, help and encouragement over all the years.

I hope the revised edition will be enjoyed as much as the earlier version, and that you will soon have new favourites to add to your present ones.

John Pitts 2004

# Contents

## Acknowledgements

The publishers would like to thank the following for permission to use their copyright material: "The Fireman's Not For Me" (MacColl)
© Stormking Music Inc, Administered in the UK & Eire by Harmony Music Ltd, Onward House, 11 Uxbridge Street, London W8 7TQ.
All rights reserved. "Down In Bethlehem" words and music by Jan Holdstock.

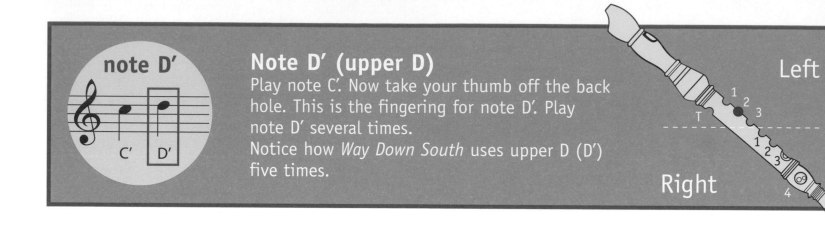

## Note D' (upper D)

Play note C'. Now take your thumb off the back hole. This is the fingering for note D'. Play note D' several times.

Notice how *Way Down South* uses upper D (D') five times.

# Way Down South

Say and clap the words.
Then play the tune.

Way down south where ban - a - nas grow, A grass - hop - per stepped on an el - e - phant's

toe. The el - e - phant said with tears in his eyes, "Pick on some-bod- y your own size".

# London's Burning

Count 1 - 2 and play on count 3.

A — Lon-don's burn - ing, Lon-don's burn - ing.

B — Fetch the en - gines, fetch the en - gines.

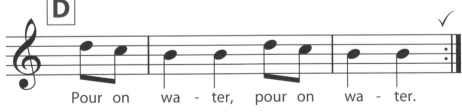

C — Fire, fire! Fire, fire!

D — Pour on wa - ter, pour on wa - ter.

**Class activity**
When you know this tune well, you can play it as a round in 2, 3 or 4 parts, or some **singers** can be Group 1 (and 3) with **recorders** as Group 2 (and 4).

## Ostinato accompaniment

You can use the first line of the round as an ostinato accompaniment (repeating pattern). Play it on a xylophone. Let the ostinato play twice before the singers and recorders join in. Later you could add line 3 as another ostinato on a chime bar, and line 4 on a glockenspiel.

# Amazing Grace

Remember to tongue-slur where a curved line joins **different** notes (slurred).

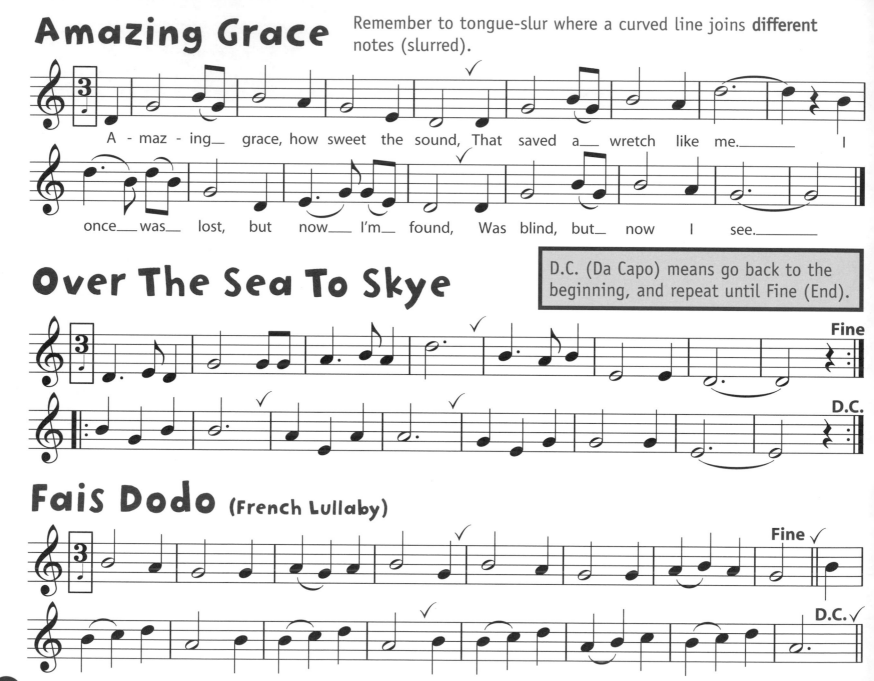

A - maz - ing_ grace, how sweet the sound, That saved a_ wretch like me.___ I

once_ was_ lost, but now_ I'm_ found, Was blind, but_ now I see.___

# Over The Sea To Skye

D.C. (Da Capo) means go back to the beginning, and repeat until Fine (End).

Fine

D.C.

# Fais Dodo (French Lullaby)

Fine

D.C.

6

Remember, both sound the same.

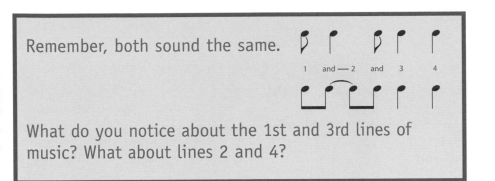

1  and — 2  and  3  4

What do you notice about the 1st and 3rd lines of music? What about lines 2 and 4?

# Cherry Tree Rag

See *Recorder from the Beginning* **Blues, Rags and Boogies** for other similar pieces.

# Hollow Elm Tree

**Class activity**

Both halves of this tune can be played or sung at the same time. So when you know the tune well, split into two groups.

Group 1 starts at A and plays all the way through. Group 2 starts at B. When they reach the end they go straight back to A and play up to B again. Group 1 can be **singers**.

Count 1-2-3 and play on count 4.

A
From out the hol - low elm tree, the owl's shrill cry we hear;

And from the dis - tant for - est the cuc - koo ans - wers clear.

B
"Cuc - koo, cuc - koo", he sings with might and main.

"Cuc - koo, cuc - koo, the spring is here a - gain".

# La Mourisque

Remember to say "tut" to tongue the staccato notes.

Ask a friend to play this ostinato rhythm as an accompaniment. It is best to use a **tambour**, like a tambourine, but with no jingles. Either use a beater or your fingers to tap out the rhythm. Make sure you bounce your hand straight off after tapping, so the sound is not muffled.

## Note F♯ (F sharp)

Play note G, and keep your fingers in position. Now put the middle two fingers of your right hand on the holes shown in the diagram. This is the fingering for F♯. Play this note several times. The music below shows where to play note F♯.

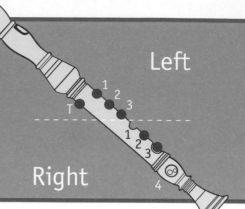

Left

Right

# Zulu Lullaby

Some tunes use note F♯ (F sharp) instead of note F all the way through. Then, instead of writing the sharp sign (♯) in front of each note F, we place it at the beginning of the stave on the top line, which is also the note F.

This turns every F into F♯, including those written in the bottom space. To help you this time there are some (♯) reminders written in.

Sharp (♯) or flat (♭) signs placed at the beginning of a stave are called the **Key Signature**.

# Sinner Man

Oh, sin - ner man, where you gon - na run to? Oh, sin - ner man,

where you gon - na run to? Oh, sin - ner man, where you gon - na

run to? All on that day.

# Now All The Forests Are At Rest (Old German hymn)

Take care to obey the **Key Signature.** In this tune it turns each F into F♯.

## Time Signatures

The number on the stave just before the first note of a tune is called the Time Signature.
The number at the top tells us how many conductor's beats there are in each bar.
If we do as the Time Signature tells us, we can conduct the band for any tune.

### Class activity
Try to conduct a tune whilst someone plays it.

First practise your conducting using the shapes given here. Count the beats as you conduct them.

When you are ready, turn back to the full tunes. Always count and conduct for one bar before the players join in. This helps them begin together. Use a pencil for a baton!

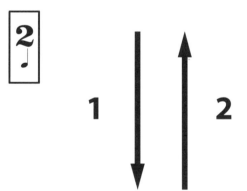

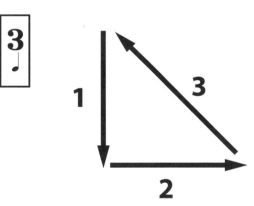

# Sinner Man (Page 11)

Oh, sin-ner man, where you gon-na run to?

# Fais Dodo (Page 6)

# Pokare Kare   Maori Song

This song is about some Maoris who are on a hunting trip, away from their families.

The tune and descant both use exactly the same rhythm. When you are playing in two parts, always listen carefully.

Are you playing in time together? Is your part louder than the other? It shouldn't be!

# Descant

## More About Time Signatures

The shape for conducting four beats in a bar is hard to remember.
Think of a sailing ship.

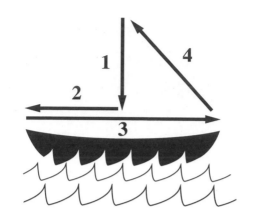

1   Down  (down the mast)
2   Back  (to the back of the boat)
3   Front (to the front of the boat)
4   Up    (up the sail)

Count four beats in a bar and practise conducting this shape.

Later you can take turns to conduct *Good King Wenceslas*, whilst others play the tune. Take care to keep conducting and counting during the long notes.

# Good King Wenceslas

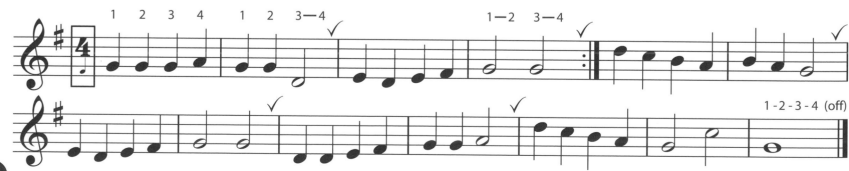

16

Another tune to play and then conduct.
Remember the Time Signature tells us how many
**conductor's beats** there are in each full bar, not
how many notes there are.

For duets and extra tunes using the notes met so far,
see *Recorder Duets from the Beginning* **Book 1** and
*Recorder from the Beginning* **Tune Book 2**.

# Down In Bethlehem*

Lit - tle   ba - by wrapped in white,   Sleep-ing   in   the can - dle light,   Mar - y watch-ing thro' the night,

Down in Beth-le -hem. (Chorus) Far   a - way,   Far   a - way,   Je-sus came to Earth on   Christ-mas Day.

*Extra verses are given in the Teacher's Book.

Not all tunes start on the strong beat at the
beginning of the bar. Some start on a weak beat
at the end of a bar. This is called an **anacrusis**.

Then we must count the rest of the bar before
we begin. Turn back and play these tunes again,
counting the beats before you begin.

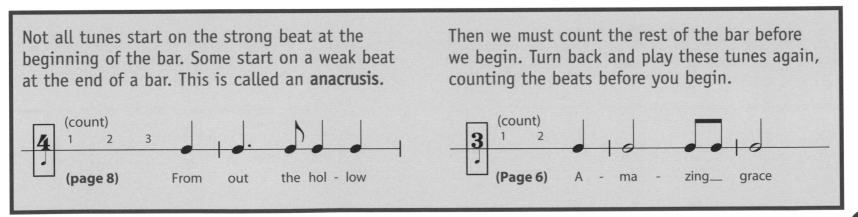

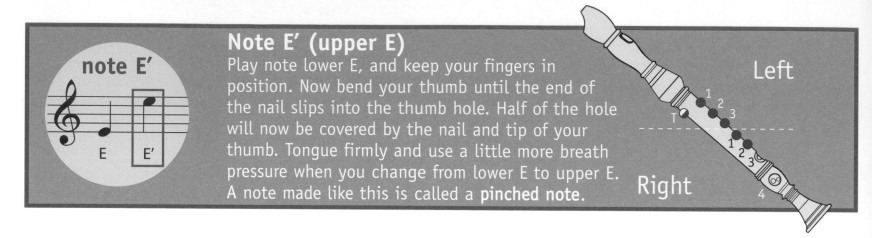

### Note E' (upper E)

Play note lower E, and keep your fingers in position. Now bend your thumb until the end of the nail slips into the thumb hole. Half of the hole will now be covered by the nail and tip of your thumb. Tongue firmly and use a little more breath pressure when you change from lower E to upper E. A note made like this is called a **pinched note**.

# Cascadura Beguine

# My Bonnie Lies Over The Ocean

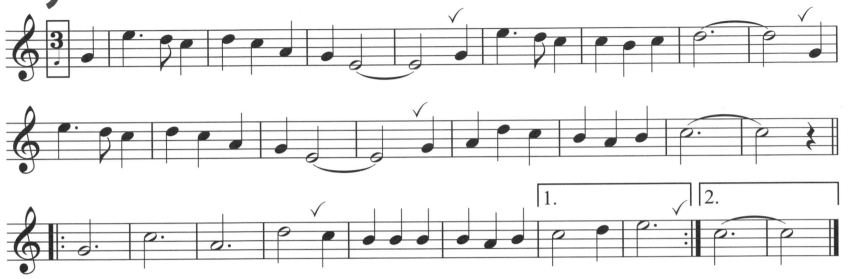

# An Eriskay Love Lilt

In the next tune, notice how the first two bars of lines 1 and 2 are the same. Is the second half of line 2 used anywhere else?

Remember that a dot above or below a note makes the note **staccato** or cut off short.

To play staccato say "tut". When you play the tune, be careful to tongue the staccato and slurred notes correctly.

# The Lord Mayor's Parade

tut  tut  tu_____  tut  tut  tu

20

The next song uses two new rhythm patterns, ♪♫ and ♪♪♪. First, say the words and clap the rhythms of (a) and (b).

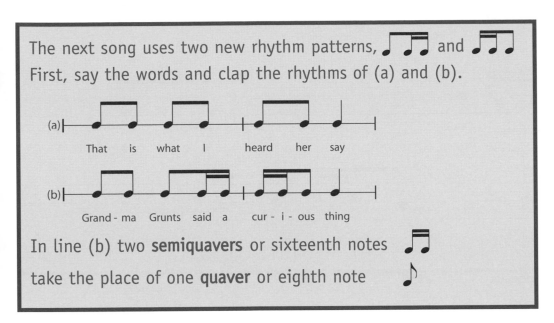

(a)

That    is    what    I    heard    her    say

(b)

Grand - ma    Grunts    said    a    cur - i - ous    thing

In line (b) two **semiquavers** or sixteenth notes ♬

take the place of one **quaver** or eighth note ♪

# Grandma Grunts

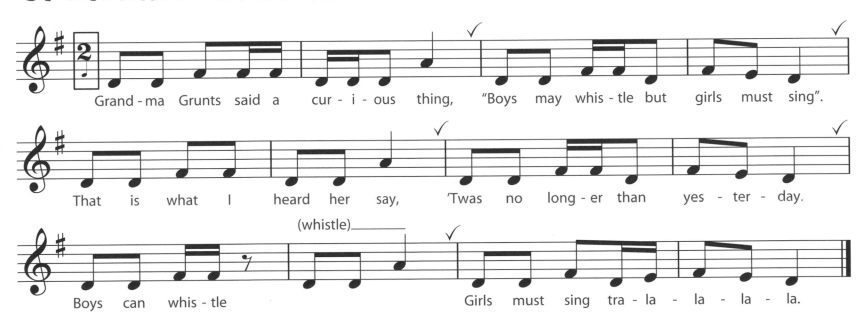

Grand - ma    Grunts    said    a    cur - i - ous    thing,    "Boys    may    whis - tle    but    girls    must    sing".

That    is    what    I    heard    her    say,    'Twas    no    long - er    than    yes - ter - day.

(whistle)

Boys    can    whis - tle                    Girls    must    sing    tra - la - la - la - la.

# Skip To My Lou

Lou, lou, skip to my lou, Lou, lou, skip to my lou,

Lou, lou, skip to my lou, skip to my lou my dar - ling.

The next tune uses two new rhythms, ♪♪♪♪ and ♪.♪
Can you find them in the tune?
See how four **semiquavers** (sixteenth notes) take the time of the first crotchet (quarter note) beat. Try to clap all the first bar as you say the words.

Here is an exercise to help you learn the other new rhythm.

First play this:

(a)

Play again but hold on the tied note:

(b)

Here is another way to write (b). The dot after the note makes the note half as long again, so (b) and (c) should sound exactly the same.

(c)

22

# Little Red Wagon

Rid-ing up and down in the lit-tle red wag-on Rid-ing up and down in the lit-tle red wag-on,

Rid-ing up and down in the lit-tle red wag-on, Won't you be my dar-ling?

**Class activity**
Partner Songs. The tunes of *Skip To My Lou* and *Little Red Wagon* will fit together.

Split up into two groups and try to play both tunes at the same time! Someone must count 1-2 so that you all begin together.

## Singers

A group of singers can perform one tune whilst recorders play the other tune. Then change over.

# Gavotte Handel

Take care to play the slurred notes smoothly.

What do you notice about line 2 of the music?

Both these tunes begin with the end of a bar (anacrusis). Count 1-2 and play on count 3.
Even though the key signature contains a C#, there are no C# notes in the tune *Kum Ba Ya*.

# Kum Ba Ya

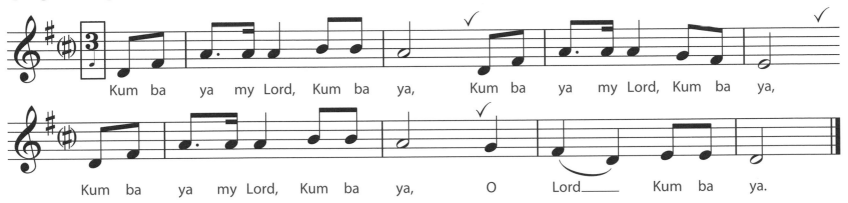

Kum ba ya my Lord, Kum ba ya, Kum ba ya my Lord, Kum ba ya,

Kum ba ya my Lord, Kum ba ya, O Lord___ Kum ba ya.

# Clementine

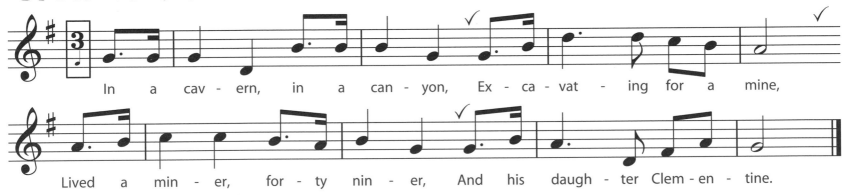

In a cav - ern, in a can - yon, Ex - ca - vat - ing for a mine,

Lived a min - er, for - ty nin - er, And his daugh - ter Clem - en - tine.

**Chorus** (same tune)
Oh, my darling, Oh, my darling,
Oh, my darling Clementine!
You are lost and gone forever,
Dreadful sorry, Clementine.

**Anacrusis (reminder)**
An incomplete bar at the beginning of a tune is called an **anacrusis**. Then the music starts on a weak beat instead of a strong one. Notice that the last bar of the tune is also incomplete. Add this to the anacrusis and it makes a full bar.

## Playing the tied notes

First play this:
Accent the note B marked >

Now tie (join) both B notes together.

# Woofenbacker's Boogie

# I Like The Flowers

**Class activity**

A **Round** to play and/or sing in 2, 3 or 4 parts.

When you can play the tune well, try it in two groups. Group 1 begins. When they reach letter **B** on the music, Group 2 starts to play from the beginning. Each group plays all the way through twice.

To perform the round in three parts, Group 3 starts from the beginning when Group 2 reaches letter **B**.

To perform the round in four parts, Group 4 starts from the beginning when Group 3 reaches letter **B**.

I like the flow – ers, I like the daff – o – dils,

I like the moun – tains, I like the roll – ing hills.

I like the fire – side, when all the lamps are low,

Last time only

Boom – ter - arr – ah, boom – ter – arr – ah, boom – ter - arr – ah, boom – ter - arr – ah, Boom!

# Land Of The Silver Birch

**Class activity**

This tune can be performed as a round in two parts

Group 2 begins when Group 1 reaches **B**. Group 1 can be singers.

**A** Land of the sil - ver birch, home of the beav - er, Where still the might - y moose

**B** wan - ders at will, Blue lake and rock - y shore, I will re - turn once more.

Hi, hi - ya hi - ya, hi, hi - ya hi - ya, hi, hi - ya hi - ya hi,_____ Hi - ya.

2nd time only

# Ten Green Bottles

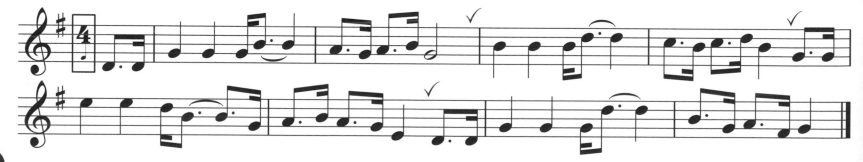

# Cossack Dance

**-** is a **minim** (half note) **rest** worth two beats.

To continue

To finish **Fine**

**D.C. al Fine**

The sign ⌢ means **Pause.** The note (or rest) under this sign must be lengthened. A total length of about double the normal value is usually right.

# Kalinka

**Fine**

**D.C.**

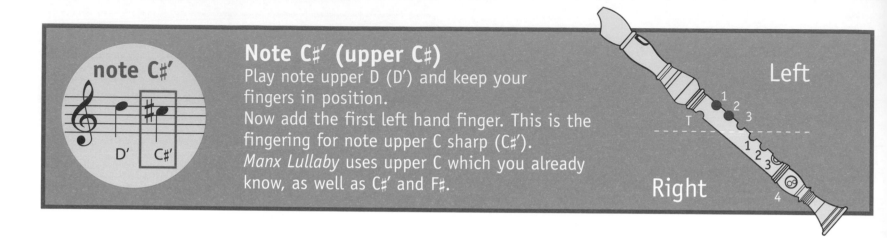

**Note C#' (upper C#)**

Play note upper D (D') and keep your fingers in position.

Now add the first left hand finger. This is the fingering for note upper C sharp (C#').

*Manx Lullaby* uses upper C which you already know, as well as C#' and F#.

# Manx Lullaby

# Boogie Blues

The Key Signature tells us to play notes F sharp (F♯) and C sharp (C♯) all the way through this tune. But in bars 4, 5 and 6 there is a **natural** sign (♮) telling us to play note C natural (C♮) instead, just in these bars.

This piece appears as a duet in *Recorder Duets from the Beginning* **Book 1.**

# Kookaburra

A **round** in two, three or four parts.

**A** Kook-a-bur-ra sits in an old gum tree,___

**B** Mer-ry mer-ry king of the bush is he___

**C** Laugh Kook-a-bur-ra, laugh Kook-a-bur-ra,

**D** Gay your life will be.

1 He sits there in the gum tree

2 Sit-ting there, in the tree, where's the food?

Singers can be one or more groups against the recorders.

## Ostinatos

Here are two ostinato patterns to use as accompaniments. Use a xylophone and a glockenspiel.

Try to begin like this:

Ostinato 1 begins and plays twice before Ostinato 2 joins in.

Ostinato 2 joins in and plays twice before Group 1 joins in.

# Tzena

**Class activity**

Both halves of this song can be performed at the same time.

When you know the tune well, split into 2 groups. Both groups start off together and perform the sections as follows:

Group 1     Chorus, Verse, Chorus
Group 2     Chorus, Chorus, Verse

Everyone should stop at the same time!

Singers can be either Group 1 or Group 2 – try it!

**Chorus**

Tze - na, Tze - na, Tze - na, Tze - na, can't you hear the rhy - thm call - ing, Run_____ and meet me there.

Tze - na, Tze - na, Tze - na, Tze - na, can't you hear the rhy - thm call - ing, Run_____ and meet me there.

**Verse**

Tze - na, Tze - na, can you hear the mu - sic? We will all be there to join the danc - ing. Come and join us, danc - ing to the mu - sic, Run on down and meet me there.

The **Tango** is a dance from Argentina, a country in South America.

A Tango always uses the rhythm ♩. ♪♩ ♩

How many times is this rhythm used in the dance tune here?

Look out for the Upper Es and C♯s.

# Tango Chacabuco

**Not too fast**

For more duets see *Recorder Duets from the Beginning* **Books 1, 2 and 3.**

Learn to play the tune first. Then learn the accompaniment.

Later, you and a friend can play both parts at once. You can also play along with the CD accompaniment.

# Incey Wincey Spider

The words of this rhyme will help you learn some new rhythm patterns that skip along.

Say and clap the words, then play the tune.

In - cey win - cey spi - der Climb - ing up the wat - er spout.

Down came the rain And washed the spi - der out.

Out came the sun And dried up all the rain, So

In - cey win - cey spi - der Climbed the spout a - gain.

The Time Signature $\frac{6}{8}$ means there are six quavers (eighth notes) in each bar. We use this for skipping tunes such as *Incey Wincey Spider*.
In slower skipping tunes the six quavers ♪♪♪♪♪♪ are counted in two groups of three. But in quicker tunes like *Row, Row, Row Your Boat*, we count them as two dotted crotchets (dotted quarter notes).

Count and clap the tune below before you play it. Then try the quicker tunes on the next page.

# What Would You Do?

What would you do if you had a cow, Who
nev - er said "Moo" but pre - ferred a "Bow - wow", Who
played the gui - tar and lived in a stye, And
put on gal - osh - es to keep her feet dry?

# Row, Row, Row Your Boat

When you can play the tune well, use the explanation on page 27 to perform in two or more groups.

This is another round that will fit in either 2, 3 or 4 parts.

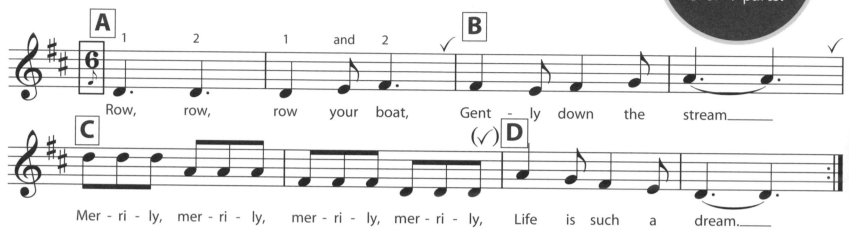

Row, row, row your boat, Gent - ly down the stream___

Mer - ri - ly, mer - ri - ly, mer - ri - ly, mer - ri - ly, Life is such a dream.___

# Haul Away Joe (Shanty)

Way, haul a - way___ We'll haul a - way the bow - lin', So

Way, haul a - way___ We'll haul a - way Joe.

# Portuguese Dance

Notice how the music from the beginning up to A is the same as from B to the end.

# The First Nowell

Includes C#'

For carols using recorders and voices see *Recorder from the Beginning* **Christmas Songbook**

# God Rest You Merry, Gentlemen

Includes E'

# Unto Us A Boy Is Born

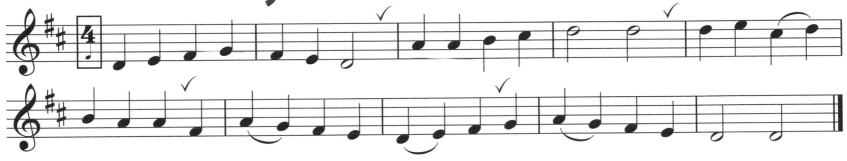

# The Child's Carol

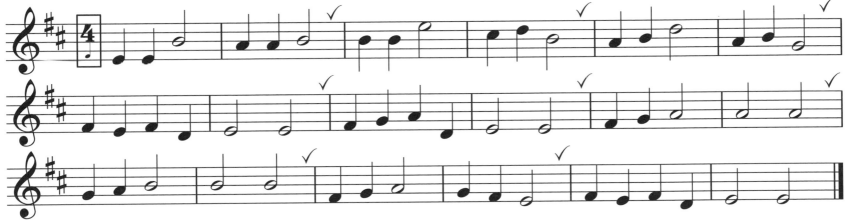

# A Child This Day Is Born

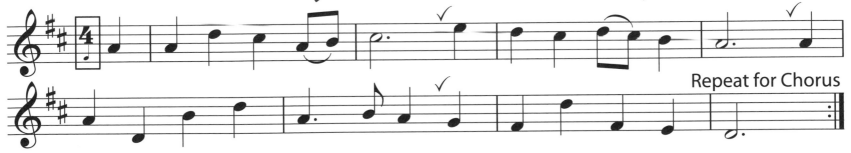

Repeat for Chorus

**Note C**
Play note lower D and keep your fingers in position. Now add your right hand little finger. Cover both small holes at the same time. Now tongue and blow very gently. This is the fingering for note lower C, the lowest note on the recorder.

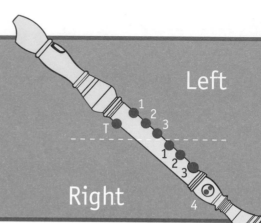

Left

Right

All the holes on your recorder should be covered. If the note doesn't sound correctly, make sure all your fingers are flat and covering all the holes. Tongue and blow very gently.

# Barnyard Song

Practise the last bar of the first line before you play the tune.

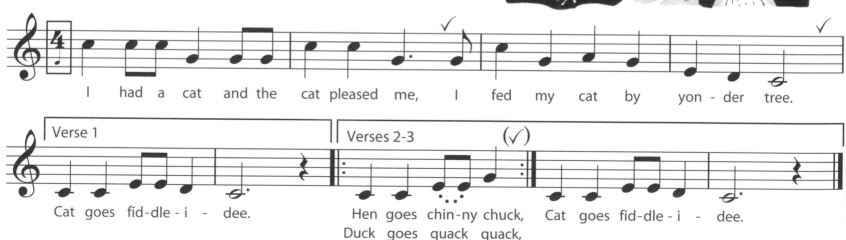

I had a cat and the cat pleased me, I fed my cat by yon-der tree.

Verse 1

Cat goes fid-dle-i-dee.

Verses 2-3

Hen goes chin-ny chuck, Cat goes fid-dle-i-dee.
Duck goes quack quack,

# The Fireman's Not For Me

Here are two more tunes which use lower C.

# Old Joe Clark

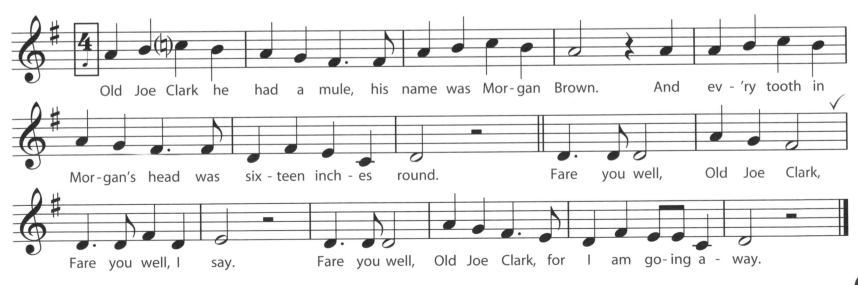

Old Joe Clark he had a mule, his name was Mor-gan Brown. And ev-'ry tooth in

Mor-gan's head was six-teen inch-es round. Fare you well, Old Joe Clark,

Fare you well, I say. Fare you well, Old Joe Clark, for I am go-ing a-way.

How many of these notes can you see?
Lower C; upper E; upper C♯

# The Ash Grove

# Old Paint

For more tunes using lower C and upper E see *Recorder from the Beginning* **Tune Book 2.**

**Chorus**                                                    **Fine**

Good - bye    Old    Paint,    I'm   a    leav - ing    Chey - enne.

**Verse**

My    foot's    in    the    stir - rup,    my    po - ny    won't    stand.____

                                                                   **D.C.**

I'm    off    to    Mon - ta - na,    I'm    leav - ing    Chey - enne.____

# Botany Bay     The verse and chorus both use the same tune.

# Scarborough Fair

Includes C#' and E'

# One More River

# Polonaise Polish dance

# CD Book 2

The accompaniment CD provides a model recorder version of each tune from the Pupil's Book. This is followed by an interesting and lively accompaniment which will provide pleasure in the practice of even the simplest of tunes.

Each piece is played first on an unaccompanied recorder, followed by an accompanied version. The accompanied version begins with an introduction as in the Teacher's Book and is then played twice. The introduction recurs as a link to the second accompanied playing. The music is arranged so that the tune can still clearly be heard by recorder players playing along with the CD.

Backing tracks arranged by CN Productions.
Solo recorder by Andy Findon.
Voice-over by John Pitts.
CD recorded, mixed and mastered by Jonas Persson.

# CD Track Listing

| | |
|---|---|
| 1 | Tuning note A |
| 2-3 | Way Down South |
| 4-5 | Amazing Grace |
| 6-7 | Over The Sea To Skye |
| 8-9 | Fais Dodo |
| 10-11 | Cherry Tree Rag |
| 12-13 | The Hollow Elm Tree |
| 14-15 | La Mourisque |
| 16-17 | Zulu Lullaby |
| 18-19 | Sinner Man |
| 20-21 | Now All The Forests |
| 22-23 | Pokare Kare |
| 24 | Pokare Kare descant (Recorder only) |
| 25-26 | Good King Wenceslas |
| 27-28 | Down In Bethlehem |
| 29-30 | Cascadura Beguine |
| 31-32 | My Bonnie Lies Over The Ocean |
| 33-34 | Eriskay Love Lilt |
| 35-36 | The Lord Mayor's Parade |
| 37-38 | Grandma Grunts |
| 39-40 | Skip To My Lou |
| 41-42 | Little Red Wagon |
| 43-44 | Gavotte (Handel) |
| 45-46 | Kum Ba Ya |
| 47-48 | Clementine |
| 49-50 | Woofenbacker's Boogie |
| 51-52 | I Like The Flowers |
| 53-54 | Land Of The Silver Birch |
| 55-56 | Ten Green Bottles |
| 57-58 | Cossack Dance |
| 59-60 | Kalinka |
| 61-62 | Manx Lullaby |
| 63-64 | Boogie Blues |
| 65 | Tzena |
| 66 | Tango Chacabuco |
| 67 | Incey Wincey Spider |
| 68 | What Would You Do? |
| 69 | Haul Away Joe |
| 70 | Portuguese Dance |
| 71 | The First Nowell |
| 72 | God Rest You Merry, Gentlemen |
| 73 | Unto Us A Boy Is Born |
| 74 | The Child's Carol |
| 75 | A Child This Day Is Born |
| 76 | Barnyard Song |
| 77 | The Fireman's Not For Me |
| 78 | Old Joe Clark |
| 79 | The Ash Grove |
| 80 | Old Paint |
| 81 | Botany Bay |
| 82 | Scarborough Fair |
| 83 | One More River |
| 84 | Polonaise |

The first track of each song is a recorder solo, and the second track is the accompaniment.

The CD accompaniments begin with an introduction, although this is not shown in the Pupil's music. Where a tune is repeated, the introduction is also repeated.

To remove your CD from the plastic sleeve, lift the small lip on the side to break the perforated flap. Replace the disc after use for convenient storage.